Baby Animals

T0052309

by Margie Sigman
illustrated by Valerie Sokolova

HAMPTON-BROWN

I like your calf.

I like your chick.

I like your lamb.

I like your kitten.

I like your duckling.

I like your piglet.

I like your puppy!